Felted
Bags, Boots

& other things

Märchenwolle *(or, in English, 'fairy wool')* is the name of a product that I discovered in Germany a few years ago... I was immediately won over by this technique for making your own felt with wool, soap and hot water. This traditional, ancient process, used by the Mongols to make yurts, today offers thousands of exciting possibilities!

It is also possible to felt wool without water. To do this, simply stitch it over a polyester foam support using special needles fitted with barbs, which are called, quite simply, felting needles. This technique is ideal for making lots of small objects, assembling felted pieces without sewing or even insetting.

With the soap technique, you will discover that wool – a rich, natural material – is alive. When the scales of the fibres are moistened in hot water and soap, they open up. You will feel them swell in your hands, then gradually close up again to form a dense, solid fabric. This material is lovely to work with, however I would recommend that you wear very thin rubber gloves to protect your hands from the harshness of the soap.

There are different qualities of wool, and some are more suited to one technique than the other. For needle felting, I recommend that you choose a wool with fairly short fibres, an irregular appearance and which is a little rough to the touch. However, for the best results with the soap technique, choose wool with fairly long, soft and regular fibres.

I hope that this book will help you discover the pleasure of working with this marvellous material and inspire you to make your own fashion accessories with even more creativity.

Cendrine

Cendrine Armani

Felted
Bags, Boots

& other things

56 Projects

SEARCH PRESS

Materials and supplies

For soap felting

A – two washing-up bowls
(one each for hot and cold water)
B – a bamboo mat for rolling up the wool
C – mosquito netting for soaping the wool
D – a towel
E – a sponge
F – household soap
G – liquid soap
H – scraps of oilcloth
I – a pair of rubber gloves
J – a wooden felting board

For needle felting

K – felting needles (with barbs)
L – a polyester foam working plate

For the designs and finishing

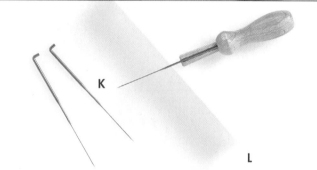

1 – carded wool in different colours
2 – a pair of scissors
3 – DMC Petra embroidery cotton no. 5 in a variety of colours
4 – assorted sewing thread
5 – fabrics in various colours and materials
6 – leather (buckskin)
7 – leather thongs
8 – knot caps
9 – zip fasteners
10 – magnetised handbag clasps
11 – handbag straps
12 – Velcro
13 – sewing needles
14 – wire cutters
15 – round nose pliers
16 – flat nose pliers
17 – small precision spring scissors
18 – compasses
19 – metal rings with a diameter of 4mm (¼in)
20 – simple mounting pins, 5cm (2in) long
21 – jewellery clasps

22 – earring clips
23 – metal mount for brooch with grid
24 – large safety pins
25 – seed beads (also known as rocaille beads)
26 – novelty beads
27 – single or threaded sequins
28 – lead glass beads
29 – beaded braids
30 – a fringed tassel mounted on a small pin
31 – a beaded motif
32 – metal chain by the metre (gold or copper)
33 – clasps
34 – metal eyelets (with assembly kit)
35 – press studs
36 – hammer
37 – erasable felt-tip pens for material and a lead pencil
38 – piping
39 – wire thread
40 – curtain cords

Not photographed
– a thermofusible glue gun and sewing machine

Flat felting

Unroll the bamboo mat over the towel.

Pull out pieces of carded wool approximately 10cm (4in) long.

Arrange these pieces vertically, in several overlapping rows.

Arrange some pieces horizontally in the same way to form a new layer.

Cover with the mosquito netting.

Add liquid soap to water at a temperature of about 50°C.

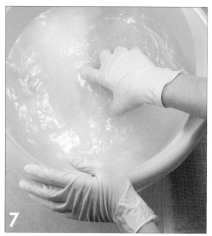

Put on the rubber gloves and soak the sponge in the mixture.

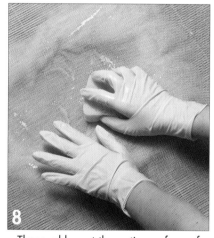

Thoroughly wet the entire surface of the wool with the sponge through the mosquito netting.

Rub the entire surface with household soap, using circular movements.

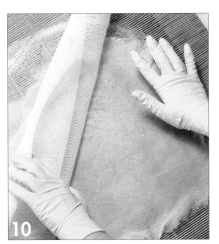

Remove the mosquito netting.

Carefully roll up and then unroll the bamboo mat with the wet wool inside.

Repeat this operation about thirty times, exerting an even pressure.

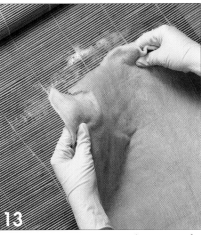

Repeat step 12, turning the piece of wool through 45° several times on both the front and the back.

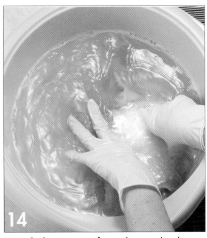

Soak the piece of wool completely in the soapy water at a temperature of about 50°C.

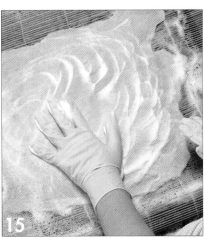

Soap the piece of wool again and massage it vigorously on both sides.

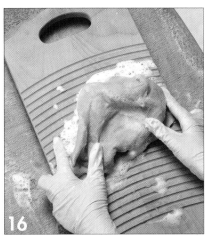

Place the piece of wool on the wooden felting board and knead it.

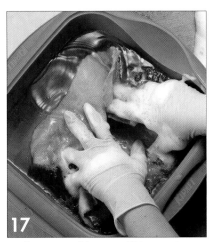

Rinse in cold water. This may be done under a tap.

Place the piece of wool on your work surface, stretch well and leave to dry flat.

Felting with template

Make your template from a scrap of oilcloth and place it on the bamboo mat.

Pull out pieces of carded wool approximately 10cm (4in) long.

Proceed as in step 3 of the flat-felting technique (see page 6). Cover the template well.

Proceed as in steps 4 to 7 of the flat-felting technique (see page 6).

Wet the entire surface of the wool thoroughly with the sponge, through the mosquito netting.

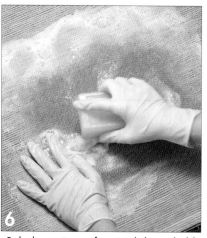

Rub the entire surface with household soap, using circular movements.

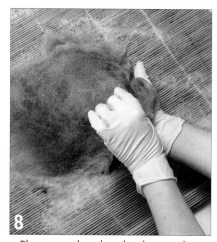

Remove the mosquito netting.

Place your hand under the template and turn over carefully.

The template is now on top of the piece of wool.

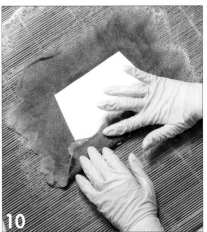

Fold the lower edge of the piece of
wool over the template.

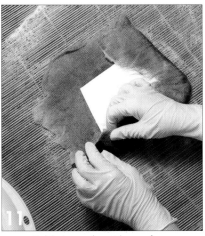

Fold down the sides to form
the corners.

Smooth carefully with your fingertips
to remove any creases.

Repeat steps 2 to 7 and turn
over carefully.

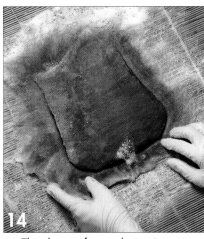

The shape of your design is now
beginning to appear.

Repeat steps 10 to 12.

Smooth the edges well
with your fingers.

Roll and unroll the bamboo mat very
carefully with the shape inside.

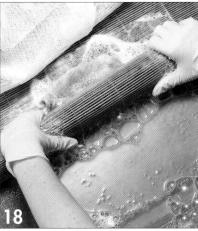

Repeat this operation several times,
exerting pressure and turning the shape
through 45° on each side.

Open the shape at the unfolded upper edge.

Turn inside out. Soak in hot water. Soap and repeat steps 17 and 18.

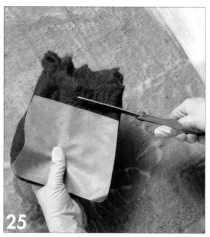

Place the template on the shape. Cut the upper edge again, leaving a margin of 15mm (⅝in).

Remove the template.

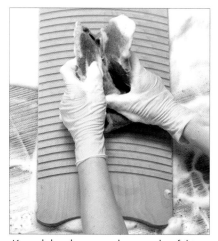

Knead the shape on the wooden felting board. Turn right side out.

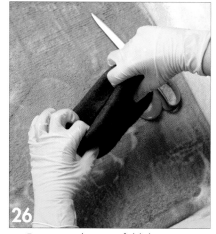

For some designs, fold the upper edge inside the shape.

Place your hand inside the shape and massage the edges well to remove the folds.

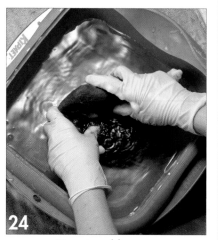

Rinse in cold water.

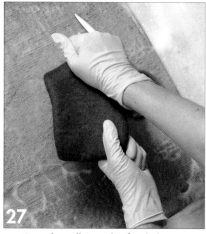

Stretch well into the final shape. Leave to dry flat.

Ball

1

Prepare a bowl of hot water (50°C) and pull out a small piece of carded wool.

2

Tease out the wool a little.

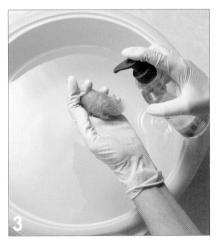

3

Moisten your hands and squirt liquid soap (2 or 3 pumps) directly on to the wool.

4

Make a ball by rolling the wool carefully in the hollow of your hands.

5

Keep the ball in your hand and plunge it into the hot water for a few seconds.

6

Roll the ball again in the palm of your hand. It should become very firm.

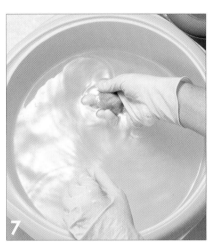

7

Plunge the ball repeatedly into the hot water to remove the excess soap and roll again.

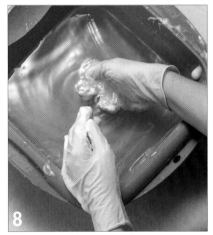

8

Rinse in cold water and press on it to remove the excess water.

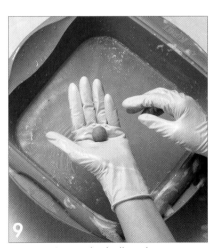

9

Leave the ball to dry.

Mixed colours

Cut-out motif

Repeat steps 1 to 4 of the flat-felting technique *(see page 6)* using one colour of wool.

Separate some fine strands in a second colour.

Arrange fine strands in the colour of your choice.

Proceed to flat felt by repeating steps 7 to 18 *(see pages 6 and 7)*.

Place the template for the motif of your choice on to the still wet piece of flat-felted wool.

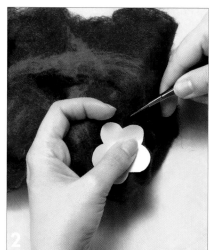

Carefully cut out the shape of the motif using the small precision spring scissors.

Snip off any imperfections.

Insets

1 Draw the motif of your choice on an item made earlier, using an erasable felt-tip pen.

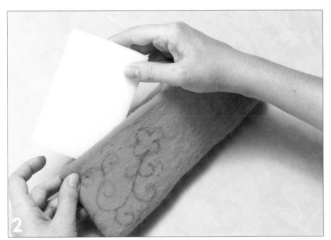

2 Place the polyester foam working plate inside.

3 Using the felting needle, stitch fine strands of wool in different colours to the outline of the motif.

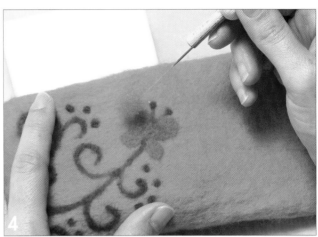

4 Use the same method to fill in certain parts (inside the butterfly).

5 You can also inset the wool on to different materials, such as denim…

… silk…

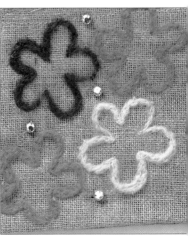

… or linen.

Pendant

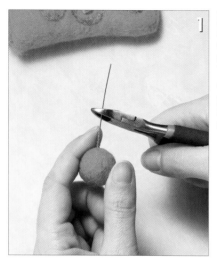

Begin by making a ball *(see page 11)* and thread on to a mounting pin. Thread six seed beads and cut the pin 1cm (½in) from the last threaded bead using the wire cutters.

Make a loop at the end of the mounting pin using the round nose pliers.

Slip this loop through the pull of the zip fastener and close using the flat nose pliers.

Embroidery

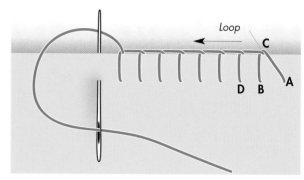

This spaced blanket stitch is worked from right to left. Thread a needle with embroidery cotton and make a knot. Bring the needle out at **A**. Insert at **B**. Pass through the loop at **C**. Pull taut and bring the needle to the front at **D**. Make sure that the spaces are even.

This stitch is also used to sew two pieces of felt together. To do this, place one piece on top of the other and stitch the two layers together.

Example of the design described on page 23.

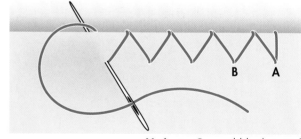

Variant – Crossed blanket stitch

Thread a needle with embroidery cotton and make a knot. Insert the needle at **A** on the top of the work. Insert the needle at **A** again. Bring the thread out at the back and insert the needle at **B**.

Example of the design described on page 48.

Lining

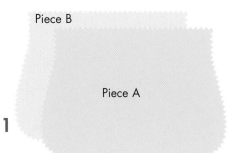

1

Cut out two pieces of cotton fabric with the same external dimensions as the chosen item, using pinking shears.

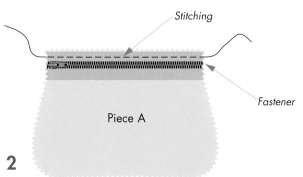

2

Stitch one of the sides of the zip fastener to the edge of piece A of the cotton fabric.

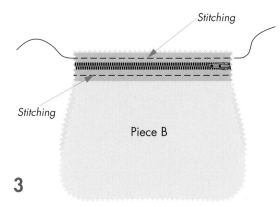

3

Stitch the second side of the zip fastener to the edge of piece B of the cotton fabric.

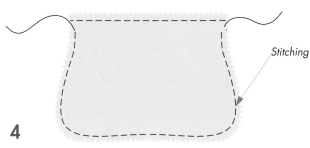

4

Sew pieces A and B of the cotton fabric together approximately 5mm (¼in) from the edges.

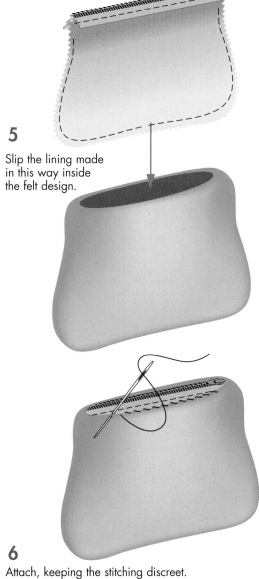

5

Slip the lining made in this way inside the felt design.

6

Attach, keeping the stitching discreet.

This example relates to the peacock blue case described on page 28.

15

Magnetised clasps

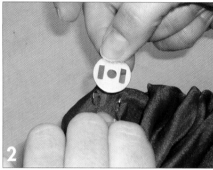

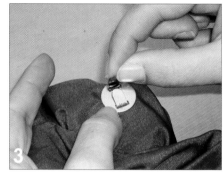

1
Snip two holes, in the required position, in the lining of the bag before closing up the opening.

2
Take one of the two parts of the clasp and slip the prongs into these holes with the fabric the right way round. Place the matching disc on the back.

3
Fold down the prongs. Proceed in the same way for the second part of the clasp on the opposite side of the bag lining.

Eyelets

1
Make a hole in the felt in the required position.

2
Place the first part of the eyelet on the support.

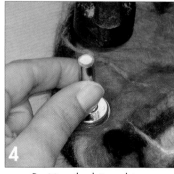

3
Insert it into the hole made in step 1. Put the second part of the eyelet in place.

4
Position the bit and tap sharply with a hammer.

Colour chart

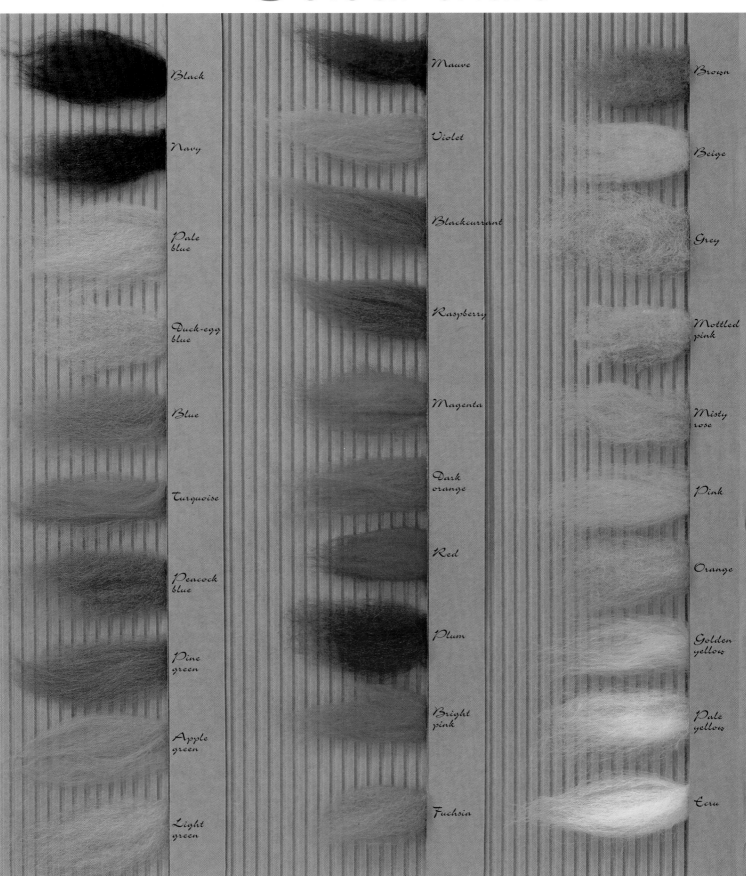

Black

Navy

Pale
blue

Duck-egg
blue

Blue

Turquoise

Peacock
blue

Pine
green

Apple
green

Light
green

Mauve

Violet

Blackcurrant

Raspberry

Magenta

Dark
orange

Red

Plum

Bright
pink

Fuchsia

Brown

Beige

Grey

Mottled
pink

Misty
rose

Pink

Orange

Golden
yellow

Pale
yellow

Ecru

Bold and Bright

Bold and Bright

Colours used

golden yellow   red   magenta   violet

wool (60g golden yellow, 20g red, 10g
magenta, 10g violet)

DMC Petra cotton no. 5 (red no. 5666
and yellow no. 5742)

20cm (7¾in) zip fastener (yellow)

24 x 32cm (9½ x 12½in) cotton fabric
(yellow) for the lining

mounting pin (gold)

6 x 2mm seed beads (yellow)

6mm lead glass beads
(4 mauve and 3 red)

1 oval lead glass bead –
18 x 12mm (turquoise)

YELLOW POUCH

Dimensions 21.5 x 15cm (8½ x 6in)

Flat felt the golden yellow wool *(see page 6)*. Cut out two rectangles measuring 21.5 x 15cm (8½ x 6in). Fit the zip fastener.

Line the pouch with the yellow cotton fabric *(see page 15)*. Sew the sides and bottom together with the red cotton using blanket stitch *(see page 14)*.

Make a pendant *(see page 14)* with a ball of red wool and the six yellow seed beads. Attach this pendant to the pull of the zip fastener.

Flat felt the red wool and cut out a rectangle measuring 7 x 6cm (2¾ x 2¼in).

Inset a strand of violet wool with a needle to form a spiral motif *(see photograph)*. Embroider this rectangle with the yellow cotton using blanket stitch and attach to the pouch with a few stitches.

Flat felt the magenta wool and cut out a rectangle measuring 5.5 x 3.5cm (2¼ x 1½in).

Sew the oval lead glass bead to the centre of this rectangle, embroider with yellow cotton using blanket stitch and attach to the pouch with a few stitches.

End by sewing on the four mauve and the three red lead glass beads.

MAGENTA PURSE

Dimensions: 13 x 8cm (5 x 3¼in)

Colours used

magenta   golden yellow   duck-egg blue

wool (40g magenta, 20g golden yellow,
10g duck-egg blue)
DMC Petra cotton no. 5 (turquoise no. 53844)
12cm (4¾in) zip fastener (bright pink)
15 x 18cm (6 x 7in) cotton fabric (bright pink) for the lining
mounting pin (gold)
6 x 2mm seed beads (turquoise)
6mm lead glass beads (4 violet, 3 red)
5 x 4mm lead glass beads (turquoise)

Flat felt the magenta wool (see page 6). Cut out two rectangles measuring 13 x 8cm (5 x 3¼in). Inset one strand of golden yellow wool with a needle to form a flower motif on one of the two rectangles, then one thin strand of duck-egg blue wool to represent the stem (see photograph).

Fit the zip fastener. Line the purse with bright pink cotton fabric (see page 15). Sew the three sides together with the turquoise cotton using blanket stitch (see page 14).

Make a pendant (see page 14) with a ball of golden yellow wool and the six turquoise seed beads. Attach this pendant to the pull of the zip fastener.

Sew the three red lead glass beads to the centre of the flower, then alternate the violet and turquoise beads along the top edge.

MOBILE PHONE POUCH

Dimensions: 5.5 x 10cm (2¼ x 4in)

Colours used

golden yellow   red   magenta   mauve

wool (20g golden yellow, 20g red, 20g magenta, 20g mauve)
DMC Petra cotton no. 5 (turquoise no. 53844 and red no. 5666)
2 x 6mm lead glass beads (mauve) – 3 x 4mm lead glass beads (turquoise)
1 x 10mm lead glass bead (mauve) – a piece of Velcro

Flat felt the magenta wool, red wool, golden yellow wool and mauve wool (see page 6).

Cut out a rectangle measuring 9.5 x 5.5cm (3¾ x 2¼in) from the magenta wool for the flap, two rectangles measuring 10 x 3cm (4 x 1¼in) from the yellow wool for the sides, one rectangle measuring 9.5 x 5.5cm (3¾ x 2¼in) from the mauve wool for the back and one rectangle measuring 13 x 5.5cm (5 x 2¼in) from the red wool for the front and bottom.

Sew all the pieces together with the turquoise cotton using blanket stitch. Edge the magenta flap in the same way.

Cut a circle (with a diameter of 20mm (¾in)) (from the golden yellow felt and edge with blanket stitch using red cotton. Sew the mauve lead glass bead in the centre and attach to the edge of the flap with a few stitches.

Sew the piece of Velcro under the flap to close the pouch.

End by sewing on the mauve and turquoise lead glass beads, alternating them along the right edge of the flap.

Bold and Bright

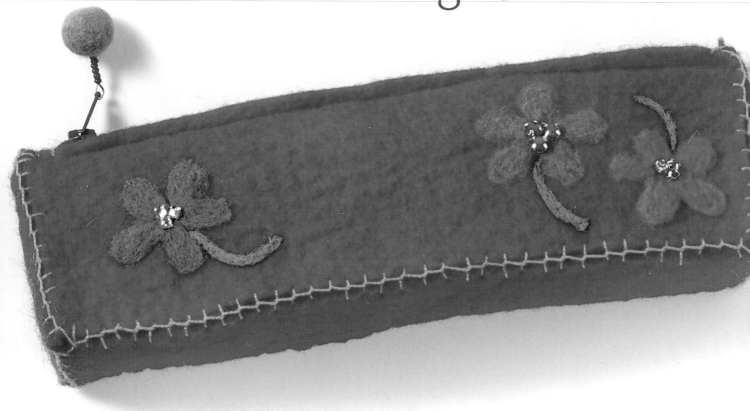

PENCIL CASE

Dimensions: 24 x 7.5 x 6cm (9½ x 3 x 2¼in)

Colours used

red   violet   orange   magenta   duck-egg blue

wool (60g red, 10g violet, 10g orange, 10g magenta, 10g duck-egg blue)
DMC Petra cotton no. 5 (orange no. 5608) – 22cm (8¾in) zip fastener (red)
30 x 25cm (11¾ x 9¾in) cotton fabric (orange) for the lining
mounting pin (gold) – 6 x 2mm seed beads (red)
3 x 6mm lead glass beads (red) – 4mm lead glass beads (3 yellow and 3 turquoise)

Flat felt the red wool (see page 6). Cut out two rectangles measuring 24 x 7.5cm (9½ x 3in) for the large sides, one rectangle measuring 24 x 6cm (9½ x 2¼in) for the bottom, and two isosceles triangles with a base of 6cm (2¼in) and a height of 8cm (3¼in), for the small sides of the case.

On one of the large rectangles, make the flower motifs, insetting small quantities of violet, orange and magenta wool with a needle (see page 13). Inset fine strands of duck-egg blue wool to represent the stems.

Fit the zip fastener. Line the pouch with the orange cotton fabric (see page 15). Sew the four sides and the bottom together with orange cotton, using blanket stitch (see page 14).

Make a pendant (see page 14) with a ball of duck-egg blue wool and the six red seed beads. Attach this pendant to the pull of the zip fastener.

Sew the three turquoise lead glass beads on to the centre of the violet flower, the three red lead glass beads on to the centre of the orange flower and the three yellow lead glass beads on to the centre of the magenta flower.

MAUVE PURSE

Dimensions: 13 x 8cm (5 x 3¼in)

Colours used

mauve   magenta   golden yellow

wool (40g mauve, 10g magenta, 10g golden yellow)
DMC Petra cotton no. 5 (turquoise no. 53844 and yellow no. 5742)
12cm (4¾in) zip fastener (mauve)
15 x 18cm (6 x 7in) cotton fabric (mauve) for the lining
mounting pin (gold)
6 x 2mm seed beads (yellow)
4 x 6mm lead glass beads (mauve)
5 x 4mm lead glass beads (turquoise)
1 lead glass bead with 10mm sides (turquoise)
1 lead glass bead with 12mm sides (turquoise)

Flat felt the mauve wool (see page 6). Cut out two rectangles measuring 13 x 8cm (5 x 3¼in). Fit the zip fastener. Line the purse with the mauve cotton fabric (see page 15). Sew the three sides together with the golden yellow cotton, using blanket stitch (see page 14).

Make a pendant (see page 14) with a ball of golden yellow wool and the six yellow seed beads. Attach this pendant to the pull of the zip fastener.

Flat felt the rest of the golden yellow wool and the magenta wool. Cut out two squares with sides measuring 4.5cm (1¾in). Sew the 12mm lead glass bead in the corner of the magenta square. Edge this square with blanket stitch using the yellow cotton. Sew the 10mm lead glass bead in the corner of the golden yellow square and edge this square with blanket stitch using the turquoise cotton. Sew the two squares to the pouch with a few stitches. Sew the mauve and turquoise lead glass beads along the upper edge of the purse, alternating them.

YELLOW PURSE

Dimensions: 13 x 8cm (5 x 3¼in)

Colours used

golden yellow   magenta

wool (40g golden yellow, 20g magenta)
DMC Petra cotton no. 5 (fuchsia no. 53805)
12cm (4¾in) zip fastener (yellow)
15 x 18cm (6 x 7in) cotton fabric (yellow) for the lining
mounting pin (gold)
6 x 2mm seed beads (yellow)
12 x 4mm lead glass beads (yellow)

Flat felt the golden yellow wool (see page 6). Cut out two rectangles measuring 13 x 8cm (5 x 3¼in). Inset a strand of magenta wool with a needle (see page 13) to form a spiral motif on one of the two rectangles.

Fit the zip fastener. Line the purse with the yellow cotton fabric (see page 15). Sew the three sides together with blanket stitch using the fuchsia cotton (see page 14).

Make a pendant (see page 14) with a ball of magenta wool and the six yellow seed beads. Attach this pendant to the pull of the zip fastener.

Finish by sewing the twelve yellow lead glass beads around the spiral.

Butterflies

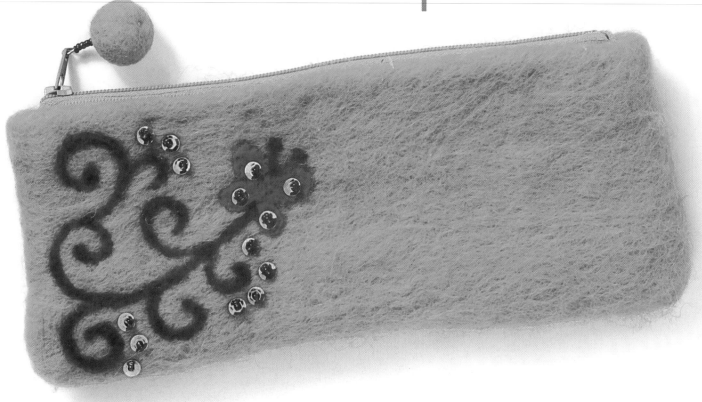

CASES
Dimensions: 22.5 x 9.5cm (8¾ x 3¾in)

Colours used

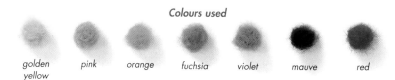

golden yellow   pink   orange   fuchsia   violet   mauve   red

Yellow case

wool (60g golden yellow, 10g pink, 10g orange)

14 sequins (orange)

20cm (7¾in) zip fastener (yellow)

25 x 22cm (9¾ x 8¾in) cotton fabric (yellow) for the lining

sewing thread (yellow)

mounting pin (gold)

20 x 2mm seed beads (orange)

Fuchsia case

wool (60g fuchsia, 10g violet, 10g mauve)

14 sequins (violet)

20cm (7¾in) zip fastener (fuchsia)

25 x 22cm (9¾ x 8¾in) cotton fabric (fuchsia) for the lining

sewing thread (fuchsia)

mounting pin (gold)

20 x 2mm seed beads (violet)

Orange case

wool (60g orange, 10g red, 10g fuchsia)

14 sequins (red)

20cm (7¾in) zip fastener (orange)

25 x 22cm (9¾ x 8¾in) cotton fabric (orange) for the lining

sewing thread (orange)

mounting pin (gold)

20 x 2mm seed beads (red)

Make a template by cutting out a rectangle measuring 24 x 11cm (9½ x 4¼in) from a scrap of oilcloth. Place the template on the bamboo mat and make the case of your choice, referring back to the felting technique on page 8.

Place the working plate inside the case and inset the motifs using a needle (see page 13).
Remove the working plate.

Sew on the sequins, threading one seed bead at the centre of each one.
Make a lining with the cotton fabric (see page 15) and fit the zip fastener.

Make a pendant (see page 14) with a ball of coloured wool that matches the case and the six matching seed beads.
Attach this pendant to the pull of the zip fastener.

Retro

Retro

PEACOCK BLUE CASE
Dimensions: 18 x 11cm (7 x 4¼in)

Colours used

peacock blue   raspberry

wool (50g peacock blue, 10g raspberry) – 15 x 15cm (6 x 6in) tweed
12cm (4¾in) zip fastener (peacock blue)
25 x 20cm (9¾ x 7¾in) cotton fabric (turquoise) for the lining
7cm (2¾in) metal chain (copper) – 1 x 6mm metal bell (copper)
1 x 4mm metal ring (copper) – mounting pin (copper)
6 x 2mm seed beads (old gold) – 1 x 15mm bead cap (copper)

Make a template from a scrap of oilcloth by cutting out a trapezium shape with sides measuring 18cm (7in) (lower edge),13cm (5in) (upper edge) and 13cm (5in) (height). Round the lower corners carefully.

Place the template on the bamboo mat and make the case, referring back to the felting technique on page 8. Make a ball with the raspberry wool *(see page 11)*.

Cut a flower shape and a leaf shape from the tweed using the pinking shears. Sew the ball to the flower and the flower to the case. Gather the middle of the leaf slightly and attach. Attach the ring to the bell and fix on to one of the ends of the chain. Secure with a few stitches to represent the stem of the flower.

Make a lining with the cotton fabric *(see page 15)* and fit the zip fastener.

Make a pendant *(see page 14)* with a ball of peacock blue wool, the bead cap and the six old gold seed beads. Attach this pendant to the pull of the zip fastener.

TWEED BAG

Dimensions: 26 x 29cm (10¼ x 11½in)
+ 68cm (26¾in) straps

200g wool (ecru)
45cm (17¾in) tweed, 1.40m (55in) wide
sewing thread (ecru)
magnetic handbag clasp (bronze)

Colour used

ecru

Make a template by cutting out a rectangle measuring 30 x 40cm (11¾ x 15¾in) from a scrap of oilcloth. Place this template on the bamboo mat and make the bag, referring back to the felting with template technique on page 8. Leave to dry and cut the edge of the bag again, 28cm (11in) high.

Cut out a tweed rectangle measuring 42 x 58cm (16½ x 22¾in). Place this rectangle on the bag, right side against right side. Sew 4cm (1½in) from the edge. Stitch the side. Fold down the fabric and slip inside the bag to make the lining.

Attach the magnetic clasp and pull out the lining again to sew the bottom.

Flat felt a strip of ecru wool *(see page 6)* measuring 100 x 10cm (39½ x 4in). Cut two strips of felt measuring 1.5cm (½in) wide and four strips of tweed measuring 100 x 1.5cm (39¼ x ½in) using pinking shears. Make two plaits with these strips to form the handles. Sew securely to the bag.

Next cut five strips measuring 30 x 1cm (11¾ x ½in) from the felt and stitch to the slightly wider strips of tweed.

Cut the edge of the tweed again using the pinking shears, allowing it to extend beyond the felt by a few millimetres. Roll each of these strips on to themselves to make roses and keep them in shape with a few stitches.

Finally cut three leaves from the rest of the felt, sew them on to small pieces of tweed using zigzag stitch and cut the edge of the tweed again using pinking shears, allowing it to extend beyond the felt by a few millimetres. Add vertical stitching with straight stitch in the middle of each leaf. Sew the roses and leaves on to the bag.

RASPBERRY BRACELET

Length: 19cm (7½in)

Colour used

raspberry

30g wool (raspberry)
16cm (6¼in) metal chain (copper)
1 metal spring clasp (copper)
20 x 4mm metal rings (copper)
30 mounting pins (copper)
6 x 15mm bead caps (copper)
12 x 10mm bead caps (copper)
6 x 8mm bead caps (copper)
6 x 8mm multifaceted beads (yellow) and
12 x 10mm multifaceted beads (pink)
6 x 12mm metal novelty beads (copper)
6 x 6mm metal bells (copper)
30 x 2mm metal seed beads (copper)
wire cutters and round nose pliers

Make six balls *(see page 11)* with different diameters (between 15 and 25mm) (½ x 1in).

Fix 12 rings **x** to the chain at intervals of approximately 15mm (½in). Make charms **a**, **b** and **c** six times and charm **d** twelve times. Cut the stems 1cm (½in) from the last threaded bead. Bend them and attach to the rings *(see diagram below)*. Next attach the six bells **e** to six rings **x** and add. Fix a ring **x** at each end of the bracelet and attach the clasp.

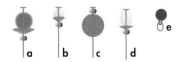

Retro

BALL POUCH

Dimensions: 17 x 13cm (6¾ x 5in)

Colours used

peacock blue   turquoise

wool (50g peacock blue, 20g turquoise)
sewing thread (peacock blue) – piece of Velcro

Make six balls *(see page 11)* with the peacock blue colour and six turquoise balls, with different diameters.
Flat felt the rest of the peacock blue wool. Leave to dry and cut out a strip measuring 18 x 32cm (7 x 12½in) keeping an irregular edge along one of the widths. Fold the strip in three. Sew the sides to a depth of 11cm (4¼in).
Turn the pouch right side out and sew the balls on to the flap, arranging them pleasingly. Sew on a piece of Velcro to close the pouch.

BEIGE CASE

Dimensions: 16 x 11cm (6¼ x 4¼in)

Colours used

beige   ecru

wool (40g beige, 20g ecru)
DMC Petra cotton no. 5 (turquoise no. 53844)
12cm (4¾in) zip fastener (grey)
25 x 20cm (9¾ x 7¾in) cotton fabric (turquoise) for the lining
sewing thread (grey) – mounting pin (gold)
6 x 2mm seed beads (pale green)
3 x 6mm lead glass beads (pale green)
5 x 4mm transparent lead glass beads
5 x 4mm lead glass beads (turquoise)
3 x 15mm marquise-cut lead glass beads (pale green)

Make a template from a scrap of oilcloth by cutting out a trapezium with sides measuring 18cm (7in) (base), 13cm (5in) (upper edge) and 13cm (5in) (height). Carefully round the lower corners.

Place the template on the bamboo mat and make the case with the beige wool, referring back to the shape-felting technique on page 8.

Flat felt the ecru wool and cut out a flower motif with five petals, two motifs with four petals and five motifs of leaves. Sew on to the case with the turquoise lead glass beads at the centre of the flowers, then sew the pale green and transparent lead glass beads between the motifs.

Add the stems of the leaves with long stitch in turquoise cotton.

Make a lining with the cotton fabric *(see page 15)* and fit the zip fastener.

Make a pendant *(see page 14)* with a ball of beige wool and six pale green seed beads. Attach this pendant to the pull of the zip fastener.

SIMPLE BRACELET

Diameter: 8cm (3¼in)

Colour used

turquoise

wool (20g turquoise)
7 x 8mm novelty beads (turquoise)
14 x 3mm multifaceted beads (beige and turquoise)
elastic thread – one large needle

Make seven balls *(see page 11)* with a diameter of 15mm (½in) from the turquoise wool.

Thread the elastic thread alternately through six balls of felt, six multifaceted beads, six novelty beads and six more multifaceted beads. Knot the threads and cut.

Colours used

peacock blue   turquoise   ecru

wool (10g peacock blue, 10g turquoise, 10g ecru)
1 pair gloves (ecru)
2 x 6mm mother-of-pearl beads (white)
12 x 4mm lead glass beads (turquoise)
sewing thread (ecru)

GLOVES

Diameter of a flower: 4.5cm (1¾in)

Flat felt the three colours of wool *(see page 6)*.

Cut out the flower motifs *(see page 12 and detail alongside)*.

Overlay the different shapes, sew the pearls and lead glass beads to the centre of each flower and attach to the gloves with a few stitches.

Retro

FLAP POUCH

Dimensions: 29 x 21cm (11½ x 8¼in)

Colours used

raspberry   *turquoise*   *peacock blue*

wool (150g raspberry, 20g turquoise, 20g peacock blue)

5 x 6mm novelty beads (turquoise)

21 x 3mm multifaceted beads (beige and turquoise)

mounting pin (gold)

12 x 4mm lead glass beads (8 yellow, 3 transparent, 1 turquoise)

sewing thread (raspberry)

Make a template by cutting out a rectangle measuring 30 x 22cm (11¾ x 8¾in) from a scrap of oilcloth.

Place this template on the bamboo mat and make the pouch, referring back to the felting technique on page 8. At step 13, arrange the wool required to produce the flap, which is 18cm (7in) in depth.

Flat felt the three colours of wool *(see page 6)* and cut out the flower motifs *(see page 12)*.

Overlay the different shapes. Sew the pearls and lead glass beads to the centre of each flower and attach to the flap of the pouch with a few stitches *(see photograph above)*.

Make a pendant *(see page 14)* with a ball of raspberry wool and six beige and turquoise multifaceted beads. Stitch this pendant beneath the large flower.

BERET

Diameter: 25cm (9¾in)

Colours used

ecru   turquoise   peacock blue

wool (150g ecru, 10g turquoise,
10g peacock blue)
68 x 9cm (26¾ x 3½in) printed velvet
6 x 4mm lead glass beads (turquoise)
1 x 6mm mother-of-pearl bead (white)
sewing thread (turquoise)

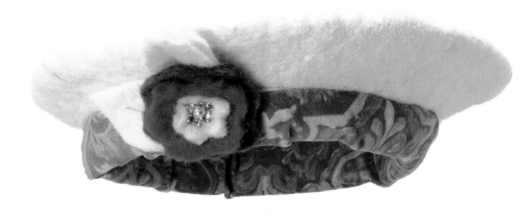

Make a template by cutting out a circle with a diameter of 28cm (11in) from a scrap of oilcloth.

Place this template on the bamboo mat and make the beret, referring back to the felting technique on page 8. Hollow the centre of one of the two sides by cutting a disc with a diameter of 12cm (4¾in).

Using a pair of scissors, make little snips measuring 1cm (½in) all the way around. Sew the strip of velvet, right side against right side, 3cm (1¼in) from the edge.

Turn the strip over to the right side. Fold over on to the edge and stitch inside the beret.

Flat felt the three colours of wool *(see page 6)*. Cut out the flower motifs *(see page 12)*.
Overlay the different shapes and sew the pearl and lead glass beads to the centre.

Cut two shapes of leaves, in the ecru colour. Add vertical stitching in the middle of each one.
Attach the flower and the leaves to the front of the beret with a few stitches.

TURQUOISE BRACELET

Length: 19cm (7½in)

Colours used

turquoise   peacock blue

wool (20g turquoise, 20g peacock blue)
16cm (6¼in) metal chain (copper)
1 metal spring clasp (copper)
25 x 4mm metal rings (copper)
23 mounting pins (copper)
6 x 8mm multifaceted beads (yellow) and
23 x 3mm multifaceted beads
(beige and blue)
6 diamond-shaped novelty beads with
12mm sides (beige and blue)
6 metal novelty beads with
10mm sides (copper)
wire cutters and round nose pliers

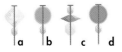

Make five felt balls with the peacock blue colour and six balls with the turquoise colour, 12mm (½in) in diameter *(see page 11)*.

Attach twenty-three rings x to the chain at intervals of approximately 7mm (¼in).

Refer to the diagram below to make charms
a, **b** and **c** six times and charm **d** five times.

Cut the stems 1cm (½in) from the last beads, bend and attach to the rings.

Fit one ring x at each end and attach the clasp.

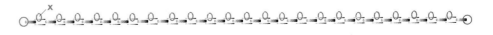

Romantic

Romantic

FLAP POUCH

Dimensions: 30 x 21cm (11¾ x 8¼in)

Colours used

blackcurrant   plum   pink   misty rose

wool (150g blackcurrant, 10g plum,
10g pink, 10g misty rose)
27 sequins (pink)
27 x 2mm seed beads (pink)
52 x 3mm multifaceted beads (violet)
sewing thread (blackcurrant)
1 erasable felt-tip pen for material

Make a template by cutting out a rectangle measuring 30 x 22cm (11¾ x 8¾in) from a scrap of oilcloth.

Place the template on the bamboo mat and make the pouch referring back to the felting with template technique on page 8. At step 13, arrange the wool required to make the flap, which is 15cm (6in) in depth.

Draw the rose motif on the left of the flap with the felt-tip pen.

Place the polyester foam working plate under the flap and inset small quantities of pink, misty rose and plum wool with a felting needle.

Sew on the sequins, threading one seed bead on to the centre of each one. Make short strings of a few multifaceted beads and attach with a few stitches (see photograph opposite).

RING

Colours used

plum   misty rose   blackcurrant

wool (10g plum, 10g misty rose,
10g blackcurrant)
1 ring mount for 10 charms (gold)
10 mounting pins (gold)
2mm seed beads (12 gold and
2 violet)
1 x 15mm metal flower-shaped
bead (gold)
5 x 4mm metal beads (gold)
1 x 8mm metal bead (gold)
2 sequins (violet)
wire cutters – flat nose pliers
round nose pliers

Flat felt the piece of plum wool (see page 6). Cut out a flower motif (see page 12) then make one blackcurrant ball and another misty rose one with a diameter of 10mm (½in) (see page 11).

Make the ten pendants (see diagram alongside) on the mounting pins. Cut them 1cm (½in) from the last threaded beads. Make loops at the ends of the pins and thread through the rings on the ring mount. Close the loops.

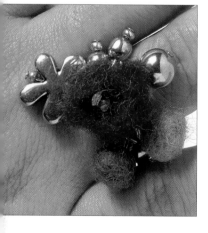

Colours used

misty rose   *plum*

wool (50g misty rose, 20g plum)
sewing thread (pink)
7 sequins (pink)
7 x 2mm seed beads (pink)
a piece of Velcro

Flat felt the misty rose wool *(see page 6)*.

Cut out a strip measuring 46 x 26cm (18 x 10¼in), keeping an irregular edge on one of the widths. Fold up the lower edge of the strip 16cm (6¼in). Stitch the sides and turn the pouch over.

Flat felt a small strip of plum wool measuring 30 x 3cm (11¾ x 1¼in). Roll up into a spiral and attach to the flap of the pouch with a few stitches.

Cut out the shape of two leaves from a piece of misty rose felt. Add vertical stitching and sew around the rose.

Sew on the sequins and seed beads.

Finish by attaching the Velcro to close the pouch.

LACE CASE
Dimensions: 16 x 10.5cm (6¼ x 4¼in)

Colours used

misty rose   *ecru*   *plum*

wool (40g misty rose, 10g ecru, 10g plum)
12cm (4¾in) zip fastener (ecru)
18 x 25cm (7 x 9¾in) cotton fabric (plum) for the lining and thread (ecru)
25cm (9¾in) lace, 35mm (1½in) wide (ecru)
mounting pin (gold) – 1 x 6mm mother-of-pearl bead (white)
6 x 6mm lead glass beads (violet)
6 x 2mm mother-of-pearl seed beads (white)
wire cutters, round nose pliers and flat nose pliers

Make a template from a scrap of oilcloth by cutting out a shape with sides measuring 18cm (7in) (base), 13cm (5in) (upper edge) and 13cm (5in) (height). Round the lower corners carefully. Place the template on the bamboo mat and make the bag, referring back to the felting with template technique on page 8. Sew the lace edging all round the case.

Flat felt the ecru and plum wool *(see page 6)*. Cut out flower motifs *(see page 12)*. Overlay the shapes, sew the large mother-of-pearl bead and lead glass beads to the centre and attach the flower to the case with a few stitches.

Make the lining *(see page 15)* and fit the zip fastener. Make a pendant *(see page 14)* with a misty rose ball and the six seed beads. Attach this pendant to the pull of the zip fastener.

Romantic

PLUM BAG

Dimensions: 32 x 28cm (12½ x 11in)

Colour used

plum

wool (200g plum)
DMC Petra cotton no. 5 (misty rose no. 53326)
66 x 35cm (26 x 13¾in) cotton fabric (pink)
110cm (43¼in) piping with a diameter of 15mm (½in) (for the handles)
magnetised handbag clasp (copper)
thread (plum)

Make a template from a scrap of oilcloth by cutting out a shape with sides measuring 35cm (13¾in) (lower edge), 26cm (10¼in) (upper edge) and 30cm (11¾in) (height). Place the template on the bamboo mat and make the bag with the plum wool, referring back to the felting with template technique on page 8.

Flat felt a piece of plum wool measuring 24 x 36cm (9½ x 14¼in) *(see page 6)*. Cut two strips measuring 36 x 8cm (14¼ x 3¼in) to make the handles, then three strips measuring 26 x 2cm (10¼ x ¾in) to make the roses. Cut out the six leaf shapes from the scraps *(see page 12)*.

Cut the piping into two and create two rings. Close by sewing securely. Roll the strips of felt around the top half of these rings.

Cut the top of the bag in a curve and place the lower part of the rings (not covered with wool) inside. Make small snips at 2cm (¾in) intervals. Fold down the felt over the lower part of the rings and stitch securely.

Felt the two handles and the top of the bag again. To do this, wet well with hot water, then soap and massage vigorously, paying particular attention to the stitches to conceal them.

Make the roses by rolling the strips into spirals and attach by sewing directly on to the bag.

Edge the leaves with large stitches using the misty rose cotton approximately 2mm (½in) from the edge.

Outline the curve of the bag beneath the handles in the same way. Sew on the leaves.

Make the lining *(see page 15)*. Leave a little gap to attach the magnetised clasp *(see page 16)* and then close this gap up with a few stitches.

SILK BAG
Width: 33cm (13in)

Colours used

plum   pink   mottled pink   misty rose

wool (10g plum, 10g pink, 10g mottled pink, 10g misty rose)
60 x 106cm (23½ x 41¾in) wild silk with rose motifs
60 x 106cm (23½ x 41¾in) cotton fabric (mauve) for the lining
magnetised handbag clasp (copper)
53 sequins (pink) – 53 seed beads (pink)
48 x 3mm multifaceted beads (violet) – sewing thread (pink)
15mm marquise-cut lead glass beads (8 pink and 8 violet)

Fold the wild silk in half. Place the pattern *(see page 62)* on to the reverse side of the fabric and cut out. Do the same with the mauve cotton fabric. Place these two pieces right side against right side and sew together. Leave a sufficiently large gap to slip in the polyester foam working plate.

Turn the bag right side out. Slip in the working plate and make the wool insets *(see page 13)* so as to fill in some parts of the flowers and leaves.

Remove the working plate. Attach the magnetised clasp and close up the gap.

Sew the sequins on to the stems of the flowers, threading one seed bead in the centre of each one.

Make short strings of multifaceted beads. Attach to the centre of the leaves with a few stitches and sew on the lead glass beads. Knot the ties to make the shoulder strap.

NECKLACE
Length: 100cm (39¼in)

Colours used

plum   misty rose   blackcurrant

wool (20g plum, 20g misty rose, 20g blackcurrant)
1m (39¼in) metal chain (gold) – 1 metal ball clasp (gold)
2 x 4mm metal rings (gold) – 42 mounting pins (gold)
11 x 15mm flower-shaped metal beads (gold)
metal beads (gold) (43 x 2mm, 11 x 4mm, 11 x 8mm)
22 x 2mm seed beads (violet) – 22 sequins (violet)
wire cutters, round nose pliers and flat nose pliers

Flat felt the pieces of misty rose and plum wool *(see page 6)*. Cut out six misty rose flower motifs and five prune motifs *(see page 12)*.

Make ten balls of violet wool with a diameter of 10mm (½in) *(see page 11)*.

Make the forty-two charms by threading the beads and pieces of felt on to the mounting pins *(see diagram above)*. Cut 1cm (½in) from the last threaded beads and bend to make loops. Pass directly through the links of the chain, leaving spaces of 20mm (¾in) between each charm, and close the loops. Fit a ring at each end of the chain and attach the clasp.

Snug Shoes for Girls

Colours used

pale yellow   orange   pink   violet

Yellow shoes A
wool (100g pale yellow, 20g orange)
DMC Petra cotton no. 5 (violet no. 5211)
6 x 4mm lead glass beads (yellow)
2 pieces of Velcro
sewing thread (white)

Pink shoes B
wool (100g pink)
DMC Petra cotton no. 5 (turquoise no. 53844)
6 x 4mm lead glass beads (turquoise)
2 pieces of Velcro
sewing thread (white)

Violet shoes C
wool (100g violet)
DMC Petra cotton no. 5 (fuchsia no. 53805)
12 x 4mm lead glass beads (fuchsia)
2 pieces of Velcro
sewing thread (white)

Flat felt the pale yellow wool (for **A**), pink wool (for **B**) and violet wool (pour **C**) *(see page 6)*.

Take the patterns on page 62 and enlarge. Cut out the top of the shoe twice, the strap twice and the sole four times from the piece of felt. Sew one shoe top and one sole together with the DMC cotton using blanket stitch *(see page 14)*. Sew the back of the shoe and the edge in the same way, as well as the strap.

Attach the strap to the shoe with a few stitches. Sew a piece of Velcro to fasten it. Stitch 5mm (¼in) from the edge of a second sole using zigzag stitching all the way round. Insert this sole inside the shoe. Make the second shoe in the same way.

For design **A**, place the working plate inside the shoe and proceed to inset the heart with the needle *(see page 13)*, using the orange colour. With the same colour, make two balls with a diameter of 2cm (¾in) *(see page 12)* and sew to the straps. Sew the lead glass beads to the hearts.

For design **B**, embroider two flowers on the top of the shoe and one on the strap with the turquoise cotton. Sew one lead glass bead to the centre of each flower.

For design **C**, cut two strips measuring 4.5 x 10cm (1¾ x 4in). Make a bow at the centre of each one. Sew three fuchsia lead glass beads on to each loop and attach the bows to the straps with a few stitches.

Children's shoe size: 8

A   B   C

Snug Shoes for Boys

Colours used

golden   pale blue   pine green
yellow

Yellow shoes A

wool (200g golden yellow)

*DMC Petra cotton no. 5 (golden yellow no. 5742
and navy blue no. 5798)*

leather (very supple)

large needle

Pale blue shoes B

wool (200g pale blue)

*DMC Petra cotton no. 5 (blue no. 5699
and red no. 5666)*

leather (very supple)

large needle

Pine green shoes C

wool (200g pine green)

*DMC Petra cotton no. 5 (pine green no. 5699
and red no. 5666)*

leather (very supple)

large needle

Take the pattern on page 62 and enlarge.

Make a template from a scrap of oilcloth by cutting out the shape of the shoe. Place on the bamboo mat and make the first shoe with 100g of the wool, referring back to the felting with template technique on page 8. Cut out the top of the shoe while still damp and make a 12cm (4¾in) slit on the front. Round the corners, fold down the sides and leave to dry.

Edge the shoe with crossed blanket stitch *(see page 14)*, using the navy blue colour for **A**, brown for **B** and red for **C**.

Place the shoe on the leather, draw the shape of the sole with an erasable felt-tip pen and cut, leaving a 5mm (¼in) margin around the shape. Sew the leather sole under the shoe with large stitches, using the colour of cotton used for the embroidery.

Make a lace with two strands of thread in the colours indicated for each design, wind it around the shoe under the flap and make a bow at the front.

Make the second shoe in the same way.

Children's shoe size: 8

A   B   C

Useful
and Practical

Useful and Practical

A

B

C

THREE PURSES

Colours used

navy   beige   pale blue   ecru   grey

Purse A
Dimensions: 17 x 10cm (6¾ x 4in)

wool (50g navy, 10g beige, 10g pale blue)
6 x 2mm transparent seed beads
2 transparent lead glass beads with 10mm sides
18 x 22cm (7 x 8½in) linen cloth for lining – sewing thread (navy)
mounting pin (gold) – 12cm (4¾in) zip fastener (navy)

Purse B
Dimensions: 18 x 11.5cm (7 x 4½in)

20 x 26cm (7¾ x 10¼in) linen cloth – sewing thread (beige)
wool (10g navy, 10g ecru, 10g beige, 10g pale blue and 10g grey)
6 x 2mm metal beads (silver) – 5 x 2mm transparent lead glass beads
mounting pin (silver) – 12cm (4¾in) zip fastener (beige)

Purse C
Dimensions: 18 x 11.5cm (7 x 4½in)

20 x 26cm (7¾ x 10¼in) denim material – sewing thread (navy)
wool (10g beige, 10g ecru, 10g pale blue)
6 x 2mm metal beads (silver) – 1 x 8mm transparent crystal multifaceted bead
6 x 5mm transparent lead glass beads – 3 x 10mm transparent lead glass beads
mounting pin (silver) – 12cm (4¾in) zip fastener (navy)

Purse A

Make a template from a scrap of oilcloth by cutting a trapezium shape with sides measuring 19cm (7½in) (lower edge), 15cm (6in) (upper edge) and 12cm (4¾in) in height. Place on the bamboo mat and make the purse, referring back to the felting with template technique on page 8.

Place the working plate inside the purse and proceed to inset the flower motif (see page 13) with the beige and pale blue wool. Remove the working plate.

Sew the lead glass beads on to each side of the flower. Make the lining with the linen cloth and fit the zip fastener. Make a pendant (see page 14) with a ball of navy wool and the six seed beads. Attach to the pull of the zip fastener.

Purse B

Cut two trapezium shapes with sides measuring 20cm (7¾in) (lower edge), 17cm (6¾in) (upper edge) and 13cm (5in) in height. Sew the sides and lower edges together on the reverse side. Turn right side out, place the working plate

inside and proceed to inset the flower shapes using a needle and fine strands of wool (see page 13). Remove the working plate and fit the zip fastener. Sew on the lead glass beads between the flowers.

Make a pendant (see page 14) with a ball of grey wool and the six metal beads. Attach this pendant to the pull of the zip fastener.

Purse C

Cut two trapezium shapes with sides measuring 20cm (7¾in) (lower edge), 17cm (6¾in) (upper edge) and 13cm (5in) in height.

Sew the sides and lower edges together on the reverse side. Turn right side out, place the working plate inside and proceed to inset the flowers with a needle (see page 13). Remove the plate and fit the zip fastener. Sew the lead glass beads in a pyramid shape on the side.

Make a pendant (see page 14) with the crystal bead and the six metal beads. Attach to the pull of the zip fastener.

HOLDALL
Dimensions: 23 x 30cm (9 x 11¾in)

Colours used

grey   pale blue

wool (300g grey, 10g pale blue)
sewing thread (beige) – DMC Petra cotton no. 5 (beige no. 5712)
75 x 32cm (29½ x 12½in) linen cloth for the lining
4m (157½in) leather thong, 10mm (½in) wide (beige)
7 x 14mm metal eyelets (silver)
2 x 12mm metal eyelets (silver)
2 x 22mm metal rings (silver)
2 metal clasps – 3.5cm (1½in) long (silver)
2 metal knot caps – 15mm (½in) wide (silver)
6 x 2mm metal beads (silver)
1 fish-shaped novelty bead (silver)
large safety pin, 7.5cm (3in) long (silver)
3 x 4mm metal ring (silver)
mounting pin (silver)

Flat felt the grey wool *(see page 6)*. Cut out a disc with a diameter of 25cm (9¾in) and sew a strip (34cm (13½in) deep and about 75cm (29½in) long) all the way around.

Close this strip at the back of the bag with stitching and turn right side out.

Attach three eyelets to the front of the bag, 12cm (4¾in) from the top, and four others at the back at regular intervals. Turn in 2cm (¾in) and edge the opening with crossed blanket stitch *(see page 14)* using the DMC cotton. Cut 1m (39¼in) of the leather thong, thread through the eyelets and pull out the two ends at the front, through the central eyelet. Make the lining from the linen cloth *(see page 15)*. Close the back with stitching and turn right side out. Sew this lining inside the bag. Attach the 12mm diameter eyelets 1.5cm (½in) from the edge of each side of the bag.

Pass a 22mm diameter ring through each of these two eyelets. Cut three 1m (39¼in) strips from the leather thong, make a plait and fix the ends with knot caps. Attach a 4mm diameter metal ring to each of them along with a snap hook. Pass the clasps through the rings on the bag to make the strap.

Make a pendant *(see page 14)* with a ball of pale blue wool and the six metal beads. Attach this pendant to the ring of the novelty bead, attach a metal ring to the other end of the bead, thread on the safety pin and pin on to the front of the bag.

Useful and Practical

PASTEL BAG
Dimensions: 21 x 32cm (8¼ x 12½in)

Colours used

pale blue   *brown*

wool (200g pale blue, 10g brown)
sewing thread (pale blue)
DMC Petra cotton no. 5 (brown no. 5434)
6 x 2mm metal beads (silver)
1 fish-shaped novelty bead (silver)
large 6cm (2¼in) safety pin (silver)
1 x 4mm metal ring (silver)
mounting pin (silver)
1 pair of bamboo handles

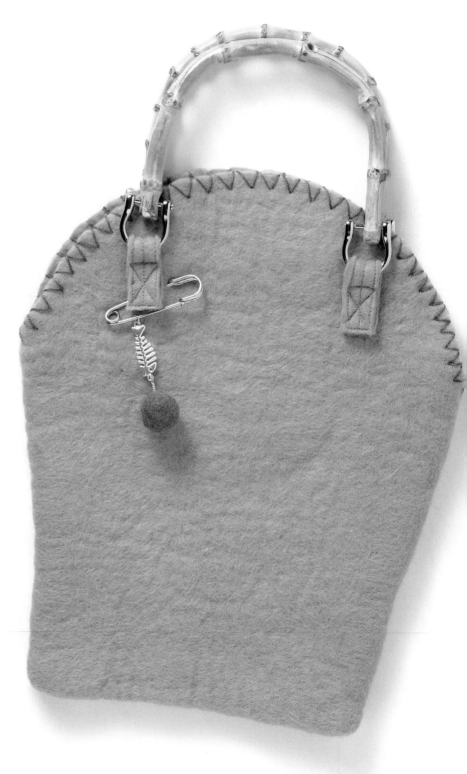

Make a template from a scrap of oilcloth by cutting out a trapezium shape with sides measuring 21cm (8¼in) (lower edge), 33cm (13in) (upper edge) and 33cm (13in) in height.

Place on the bamboo mat and make the bag, referring back to the felting with template technique on page 8.

Cut the top of the bag again, in a curve, while still damp, and leave to dry flat.

Edge the opening with crossed blanket stitch *(see page 14)* using the DMC cotton.

Cut four strips measuring 10 x 2cm (4 x ¾in) from the pieces of felt and stitch along the sides and the centre. Pass through the handle fastenings and stitch to close up. Sew securely to the bag on the right side.

Make a pendant *(see page 14)* with a ball of brown wool and the six metal beads. Fix this pendant to the ring of the novelty bead.

Attach the metal ring to the other end of the bead, thread on to the safety pin and pin to the front of the bag.

KIDS' BAGS

Colours used

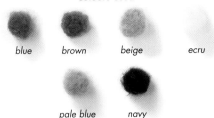

blue   brown   beige   ecru

pale blue   navy

A

Bag A
Dimensions: 28 x 30cm (11x 11¾in)

wool (200g blue, 20g brown)
sewing thread (light brown)
DMC Petra cotton no. 5 (cinnamon no. 5738)
1 x 5cm (2in) safety pin (bronze)
1m (39¼in) supple leather thong, 5mm (¼in) wide
1 pair of rope and wooden handles
22cm (8¾in) zip fastener (light brown)
60 x 32cm (23½ x 12½in) linen cloth for the lining

Bag B
Dimensions: 28 x 28cm (11 x 11in)

wool (200g blue, 10g navy, 10g ecru, 10g beige,
10g pale blue, 10g brown)
4 x 14mm metal eyelets (silver)
4 metal clasps, 5.5cm (2¼in) long (silver)
2 curtain cords (beige)
1 fringed tassel mounted on small pin (beige)

Bag A
Make a template from a scrap of oilcloth by cutting out a rectangle measuring 30 x 32cm (11¾ x 12½in). Place on the bamboo mat and make the bag, referring back to the felting with template technique on page 8. Cut the top of the bag again while still damp and leave to dry flat.

Edge the opening with blanket stitch *(see page 14)* using the DMC cotton. Cut four 10 x 2cm (4 x ¾in) strips from the felt pieces. Stitch along the sides and the centre. Pass through the fastenings of the handles and sew to close up. Sew securely to the inside of the bag.

Make the lining with the linen cloth *(see page 15)* and fit the zip fastener. Flat felt the brown wool *(see page 6)*. Cut out the silhouette of the gingerbread man *(see pattern on page 62)*, edge with blanket stitch *(see page 14)* and sew on to the bag.

Cut the leather thong into three unequal strips. Knot in the middle on to the safety pin and pin to the top of the bag.

Bag B
Make a template from a scrap of oilcloth by cutting out a rectangle measuring 30 x 32cm (11¾ x 12½in). Place on the bamboo mat and make the bag, referring back to the felting with template technique on page 8 and the mixed colours technique on page 12.

Turn in the top of the bag and attach the eyelets 8cm (3¼in) from the sides.

Knot the cords to the clasps to make the straps and pass through the eyelets.

End by fixing the tassel to the front of the bag.

B

Trendy

Trendy

FLOWER BROOCH

Diameter: 19.5cm (7¾in)

Colours used

| plum | red | bright pink | black |

wool (50g plum, 20g red, 20g bright pink, 20g black)
6mm beads (6 gold, 6 fuchsia, 6 black, 3 red)
3 x 8mm beads (red)
1m (39¼in) leather thong (black) – sewing thread (black)
1 x 35mm brooch mount with grid (silver)

Flat felt the pieces of wool, mixing the colours *(see page 12)*.

Cut out the motif for each petal six times *(see patterns on page 63)*. Sew on to the grid of the brooch mount, then sew the beads to the centre of the flower. Cut the leather thong into three unequal pieces and attach to the back of the flower with a few stitches.

SCARF

Dimensions: 14 x 96cm (5½ x 37¾in)

Colour used

plum

wool (100g plum)
3 x 15mm press studs (black)

Flat felt the plum wool *(see page 6)* to form a strip measuring 15 x 100cm (6 x 39¼in), taking care to fold the edges over themselves carefully before moving on to step 11 to obtain a neat border.

Make sure you stretch the felt piece well in the final stage to give it its final shape.

Leave to dry flat and attach the press studs.

BAG

Dimensions: 30 x 30cm (11¾ x 11¾in)

Colour used

red

wool (300g red) – sewing thread (black)
75 x 32cm (29½ x 12½in) taffeta (red) for the lining
1m (39¼in) bias binding in imitation leather (black)
leather thongs with a diameter of 3mm (⅛in)
(2m (78¾in) black and 2m (78¾in) red)
9 x 14mm metal eyelets (black)
1 pair of handbag handles (black)
magnetised handbag clasp (gold)

Flat felt the red wool *(see page 6)*. Cut out a disc with a diameter of 25cm (9¾in) for the bottom of the bag and a strip 33cm (13in) deep and about 75cm (29½in) long; sew all the way around. Close this strip at the back of the bag with stitching and turn right side out.

Attach five eyelets to the front of the bag, 12cm (4¾in) from the top, and four others at the back at regular intervals.

Cut the leather thongs in two, pass through the eyelets and bring out at the front through the central eyelet.

Make the lining from the red taffeta *(see page 15)*. Attach the magnetised clasp *(see page 16)* and sew the lining inside the bag. Sew the bias binding along the rim of the opening, across both layers (felt and lining).

Cut four 5cm (2in) strips of bias binding, pass through the fastenings of the handles and stitch to close. Sew securely to the inside of the bag.

BAG CHARM

Dimensions 5 x 8cm (2 x 3¼in)

Colours used

plum   bright pink   red

wool (10g plum, 10g bright pink, 10g red)
3 x 20mm mother-of-pearl discs (fuchsia)
1 mother-of-pearl heart – 30 x 30mm (1¼ x 1¼in) (black)
11cm (4¼in) chain (gold)
14 x 4mm metal rings (gold)
3 metal cube-shaped beads with 5mm sides (gold)
6 x 6mm metal beads (gold)
3 x 2mm metal beads (gold)
3 mounting pins (gold)
1 x 5cm (2in) large safety pin (gold) fitted with 7 rings

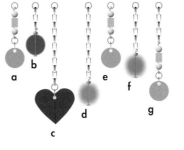

Make the seven charms, referring back to the diagram above. Fix to the rings on the safety pin. Charms **b**, **d** and **f** are made from balls of plum, bright pink and red wool *(see page 11)*.

Trendy

RING

Colours used

plum   red   bright pink   black

wool (10g plum, 5g red, 5g bright pink, 5g black)
3 square beads with 5mm sides (black)
3mm beads (4 red, 1 fuchsia, 1 dark red)
1 x 6mm bead (red) – sewing thread (black)
1 ring mount with grid (silver)

Flat felt the pieces of wool, mixing the colours
(see page 12). Refer to the patterns on page 63
to reproduce the motif of a flower, and cut out
(see page 12).
Sew the beads to the centre. Attach the flower to the
grid of the ring mount with a few stitches.

KEY RING

Length: 16.5cm (6½in)

Colours used

plum   bright pink   red

wool (10g plum, 10g bright pink, 10g red)
1 x 20mm mother-of-pearl disc (fuchsia)
1 mother-of-pearl petal – 30 x 40mm (1¼ x 1½in) (black)
1 x 27mm (1in) mother-of-pearl flower (fuchsia)
50cm (19¾in) chain (gold) – 18 x 4mm metal rings (gold)
3mm beads (1 fuchsia, 1 red)
6mm beads (2 fuchsia, 1 red)
1 x 8mm bead (dark red)
15 x 2mm metal beads (gold)
6 x 15mm sequins (gold)
3 mounting pins (gold)
1 x 3.5cm clasp (gold)

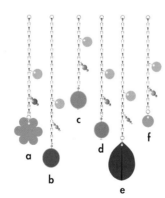

a   b   c   d   e   f

Make the six charms, referring back to the
diagram above, and attach to the ring on
the clasp. Pendants **b**, **c** and **d** are made
from balls of plum, bright pink and red wool
(see page 11).

NECKLACE

Colours used

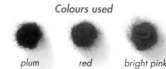

plum   red   bright pink

wool (30g plum, 20g red,
20g bright pink)
5 crimp beads (copper)
1m (39¼in) wire thread (red)
2 x 6mm metal beads (gold)
1 metal ball clasp (gold)
2 large needles
flat nose pliers

Make nine plum balls, four red balls and three bright pink
balls in unequal sizes (see page 11).

Take 60cm (23½in) of wire thread, thread one large needle
at each end and thread on the felt balls (see diagram
below). Gather the two strands, thread one crimp bead on
to them and flatten with the flat nose pliers. Cut two pieces
of wire thread measuring 18cm (7in) each. Thread and
crimp one bead at one end of each of them, pass the first
piece of wire thread through the first threaded ball and
pass the second through the last. Thread one metal bead
on each side then one crimp bead. Pass each strand
through the holes of the clasp, thread the strands through
the crimp beads again and flatten with the pliers. Cut the
threads again.

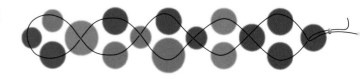

POUCH

Dimensions: 14 x 17.5cm (5½ x 7in)

Colour used

red

wool (100g red) – sewing thread (black)
1m (39¼in) cord with a diameter of 6mm (¼in) (black) – 2 x 7mm eyelets (gold)
2 braid fasteners (black)

Flat felt the red wool *(see page 6)*. Cut out a strip measuring
15 x 46cm (6 x 18in). Fold this strip in three and sew the sides to a
depth of 15cm (6in). Turn the pouch right side out.

Cut two strips measuring 17 x 2cm (6¾ x ¾in), stitch along the centre
and the sides. Attach one eyelet *(see page 16)* to each of them at a
height of 12cm (4¾in). Pass the ends of the cord through the eyelets
and make a knot to secure it.

Sew the strips on to the flap of the pouch and zigzag stitch all the way
around the opening and the flap with the black thread.

Sew on the braid fasteners to close the pouch.

FINGERLESS GLOVES

Colours used

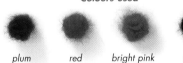

plum   *red*   *bright pink*   *black*

1 pair of fingerless gloves (black)
wool (20g plum, 10g red, 10g bright pink, 10g black)
4 square beads with 5mm sides (black)
8 x 3mm beads (red) – 4 x 3mm beads (dark red)
6mm beads (4 red and 4 dark red)
4 x 6mm stone beads (bright pink)
20 x 2mm metal beads (gold) – sewing thread (black)

Flat felt the pieces of wool, mixing
the colours *(see page 12)*.

Take the pattern on page 63 and cut
out the flower motif **a** for the shoe
jewel four times *(see page 12)*.

Sew the beads on to the centre of
the flowers *(see photograph)*.
Arrange and attach the flowers on
the fingerless gloves with a few
stitches.

SHOE JEWEL

Diameter: 8cm (3¼in)

Colours used

plum   *red*   *bright pink*   *black*

wool (20g plum, 10g red, 10g bright pink, 10g black)
one piece of leather or imitation leather,
13 x 6.5cm (5 x 2¼in) (black)
2 x 15mm press studs (black)
2 earring clips

Flat felt the pieces of wool, mixing
the colours *(see page 12)*.

Take the pattern on page 63 and cut out the motifs of
flowers **a** and **c** *(see page 12)*.
Next cut the shape of flower **b**
from the piece of leather.

Arrange the flowers one on top of the other,
beginning with **c** then **b** and finally **a**.
Fix the press stud to the centre and glue the flower to
an earring clip with the glue gun.

Make a second jewel in the same way.

Oriental

Oriental

FLOWER BROOCH

Diameter: 19.5cm (7¾in)

Colours used

fuchsia   *orange*   *bright pink*

wool (50g fuchsia, 20g orange, 20g bright pink)
6mm beads (6 gold, 6 fuchsia)
6mm stone beads (3 bright pink, 3 orange)
8mm stone beads (3 pink, 3 orange)
1m (39¼in) leather thong (bright pink)
embroidery thread (gold) – sewing thread (fuchsia)
1 brooch mount with grid (silver)

Flat felt the pieces of wool, mixing the colours *(see page 12)*. Add the gold thread at step 2 and cover partially with a light layer of wool.

Cut out each petal motif six times *(see patterns on page 63)*. Sew on to the grid of the brooch mount, then sew the beads on to the centre of the flower.

Cut the leather thong into three unequal pieces and attach to the back of the flower with a few stitches.

PURSE

Dimensions: 18 x 11cm (7 x 4¼in)

Colours used

pink   *dark orange*

wool (50g pink, 10g dark orange)
12cm (4¾in) zip fastener (pink)
25 x 20cm (9¾ x 7¾in) cotton fabric (orange) for the lining
sewing thread (pink)
28cm (11in) braid, 6mm (¼in) wide (orange)
3 x 15mm sequins (gold) – 43 x 5mm sequins (orange)
46 x 2mm seed beads (orange)
5 x 15mm marquise-cut lead glass beads (pink)
1 x 8mm multifaceted bead (pink) – 4 x 3mm beads (gold)
3 x 5mm crystal flowers (orange) – mounting pin (gold)

Make a template from a scrap of oilcloth by cutting a shape with sides measuring 18cm (7in) (lower edge), 13cm (5in) (upper edge) and 13cm (5in) in height. Round the lower corners carefully. Place the template on the bamboo mat and make the purse, referring back to the felting with template technique on page 8.

Place the working plate inside and proceed to inset the motifs with the dark orange wool using a needle *(see page 13)*. Remove the working plate, sew on the lead glass beads, sequins and seed beads, taking inspiration from the model shown.

Make the lining with the cotton fabric *(see page 15)* and fit the zip fastener. Sew the braid to the edge. Make a pendant by threading the multifaceted bead, then the gold beads and orange flowers, alternating them on the mounting pin. Attach this pendant to the pull of the zip fastener.

BRIGHT PINK BAG

Dimensions: 27 x 32cm (10¾ x 12½in)

Colour used

bright pink

wool (200g bright pink) – sewing thread (bright pink)
DMC Petra cotton no. 5 (orange no. 5608)
1 pair of handbag handles
22cm (8¾in) zip fastener (bright pink)
60 x 32cm (23½ x 12½in) cotton fabric (orange) for the lining

Make a template from a scrap of oilcloth by cutting out a rectangle measuring 30 x 32cm (11¾ x 12½in). Place on the bamboo mat and make the bag, referring back to the felting with template technique on page 8. Cut the top of the bag again while still damp and leave to dry flat.

Edge the opening with the DMC cotton using blanket stitch (see page 14).

Cut four strips measuring 10 x 2cm (4 x ¾in) from the scraps of felt. Stitch the sides and centre, then pass through the handle fastenings. Stitch to close up and sew securely to the inside of the bag. Make the lining with the cotton fabric (see page 15) and attach the zip fastener.

ORANGE BAG

Dimensions: 32 x 26cm (12½ x 10¼in)

Colours used

orange   fuchsia

wool (200g orange, 20g fuchsia)
20cm (7¾in) zip fastener (orange) – sewing thread (orange)
40 x 60cm (15¾ x 23½in) cotton fabric (fuchsia) for the lining
50cm (19¾in) beaded braid, 6mm (¼in) wide (orange)
6 x 15mm sequins (gold) – 20 x 5mm sequins (gold)
26 x 2mm seed beads (fuchsia)
6 marquise-cut lead glass beads, 15mm long (pink)
1 x 8mm metal novelty bead (gold)
1 pair of handbag handles

Make a template from a scrap of oilcloth by cutting a trapezium with sides measuring 37cm (14½in) (lower edge), 27cm (10¾in) (upper edge) and 28cm (11in) in height. Place on the bamboo mat and make the bag, referring back to the felting with template technique on page 8. Place the working plate inside and proceed to inset the rosette motif (see page 63). Remove the working plate.

Sew the novelty bead in the centre of the rosette, then seed beads with the little fuchsia sequins all the way round. Sew the six remaining seed beads and the gold sequins to the middle of the large fuchsia sequins, then the marquise-cut lead glass beads on the outside.

Cut four strips measuring 10 x 2cm (4 x ¾in) from the scraps of felt. Stitch the sides and the centre, pass through the handle fastenings and stitch to close up. Sew securely to the inside of the bag. Make the lining (see page 15) with the cotton fabric and attach the zip fastener.

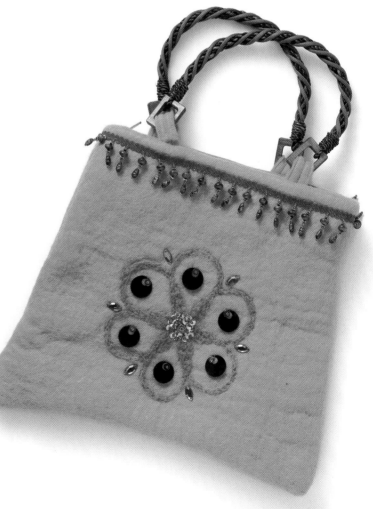

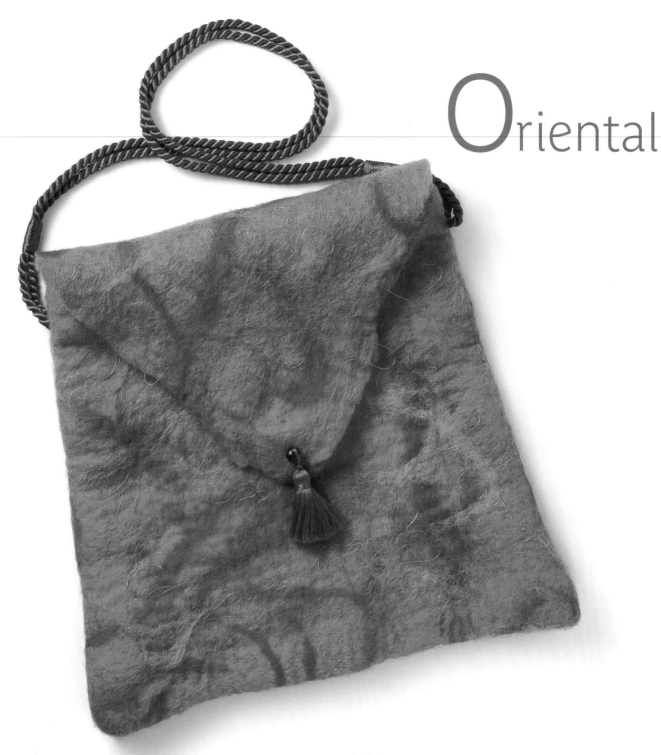

Oriental

MULTICOLOURED BAG

Dimensions : 32 x 30 cm (12½ x 11¾in)

Colours used

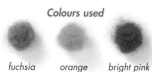

fuchsia   orange   bright pink

wool (200g fuchsia, 50g orange, 50g bright pink)
embroidery thread (gold) – sewing thread (fuchsia)
20cm (7¾in) zip fastener (orange)
40 x 60cm (15¾ x 23½in) cotton fabric (fuchsia) for the lining
piece of Velcro
fringed tassel mounted on a small pin (fuchsia)
curtain cord (fuchsia) for the strap

Flat felt a piece of felt measuring 24 x 24cm (9½ x 9½in), mixing the colours *(see page 12)*. Add gold thread at step 2 and cover partially with a light layer of wool.

Make a template from a scrap of oilcloth, cutting out a trapezium shape with sides measuring 37cm (14½in) (lower edge), 27cm (10¾in) (upper edge) and 28cm (11in) in height. Place on the bamboo mat and make the bag (referring back to the felting technique on page 8), mixing the colours as before.

Cut the piece of felt into a triangle and sew to the back of the bag to make the flap. If necessary, tuck in the gold threads with a needle.

Make a lining with the cotton fabric *(see page 15)* and fit the zip fastener.

Add the curtain cord to make the strap and the Velcro beneath the flap, then fix the tassel to the pointed end of the flap.

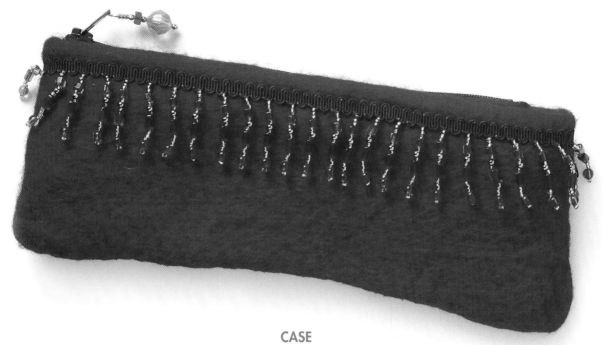

CASE

Dimensions: 24 x 9.5cm (9½ x 3¾in)

Colour used

red

wool (60g red)
20cm (7¾in) zip fastener (red)
25 x 22cm (9¾ x 8¾in) cotton fabric (orange) for the lining
sewing thread (red) – 50cm (19¾in) beaded braid
1 x 8mm multifaceted bead (pink)
3 x 2mm seed beads (orange) – 3 x 3mm beads (gold)
1 x 6mm cylindrical bead (red) – mounting pin (gold)

Make a template from a scrap of oilcloth, cutting out a rectangle measuring 25 x 11cm (9¾ x 4¼in). Place the template on the bamboo mat and make the case, referring back to the felting with template technique on page 8.

Make the lining with the cotton fabric *(see page 15)* and fit the zip fastener. Sew the beaded braid to the edge of the case.

Make a pendant by threading one gold bead, the multifaceted bead, one gold bead, the red bead, one gold bead and the three seed beads on to the mounting pin. Attach to the pull of the zip fastener.

PURSE

Dimensions: 9 x 8.5cm (3½ x 3¼in)

Colour used

dark orange

wool (30g dark orange) – 10cm (4in) zip fastener (orange)
10 x 20cm (4 x 7¾in) cotton fabric (fuchsia) for the lining – sewing thread (orange)
22cm (8¾in) braid, 6mm (¼in) wide (orange)
22cm (8¾in) threaded sequins (red) – 1 beaded motif
1 x 8mm multifaceted bead (red)
6 x 2mm seed beads (red) – mounting pin (gold)

Make a template from a scrap of oilcloth by cutting out a 10cm (4in) square. Place the template on the bamboo mat and make the purse, referring back to the felting with template technique on page 8.

Make a lining with the cotton fabric *(see page 15)* and fit the zip fastener. Sew the braid on to the upper edge and the threaded sequins below. End with the beaded motif in the centre of the purse.

Make a pendant by threading the multifaceted bead and the six seed beads on to the mounting pin. Attach this pendant to the pull of the zip fastener.

Patterns

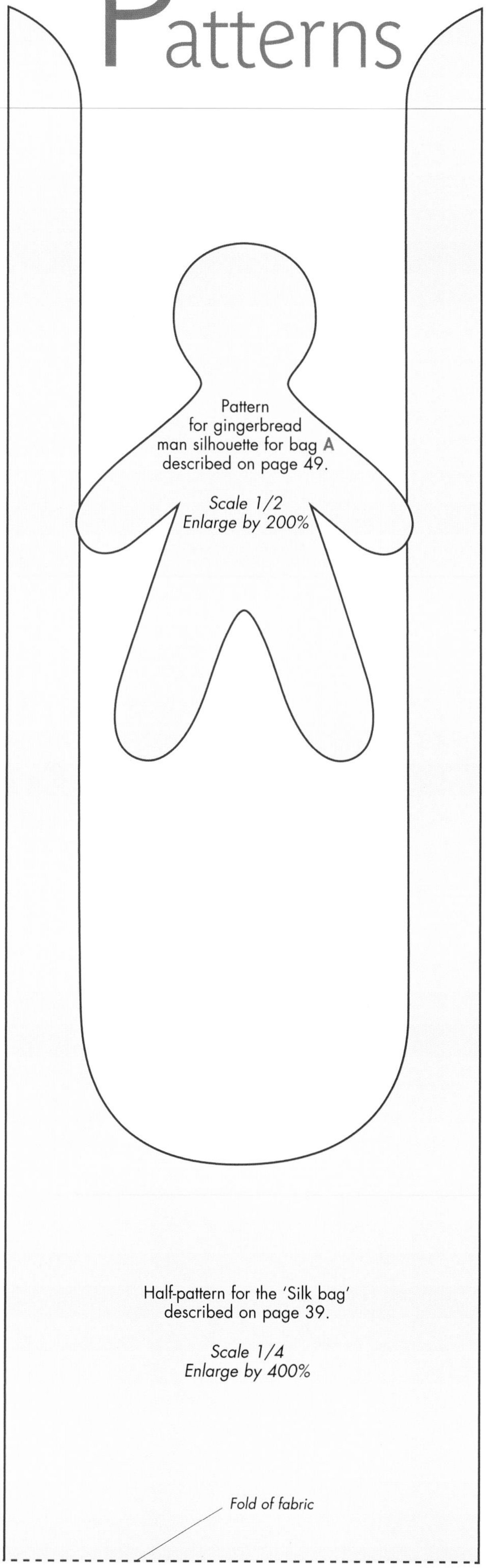

Sole

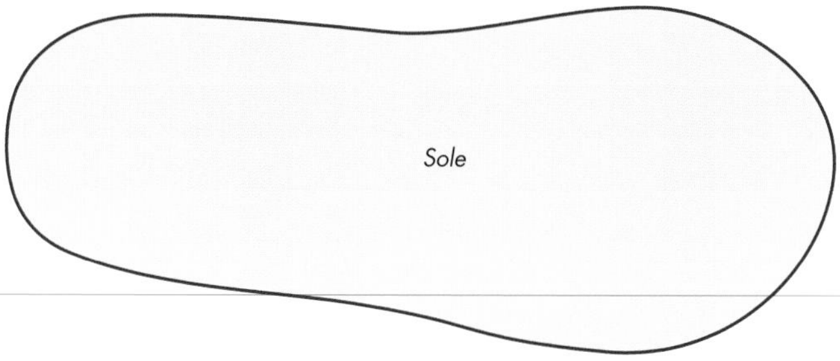

Patterns for the shoe in 'Snug shoes for girls' described on page 40.

Scale 1/2
Enlarge by 200%

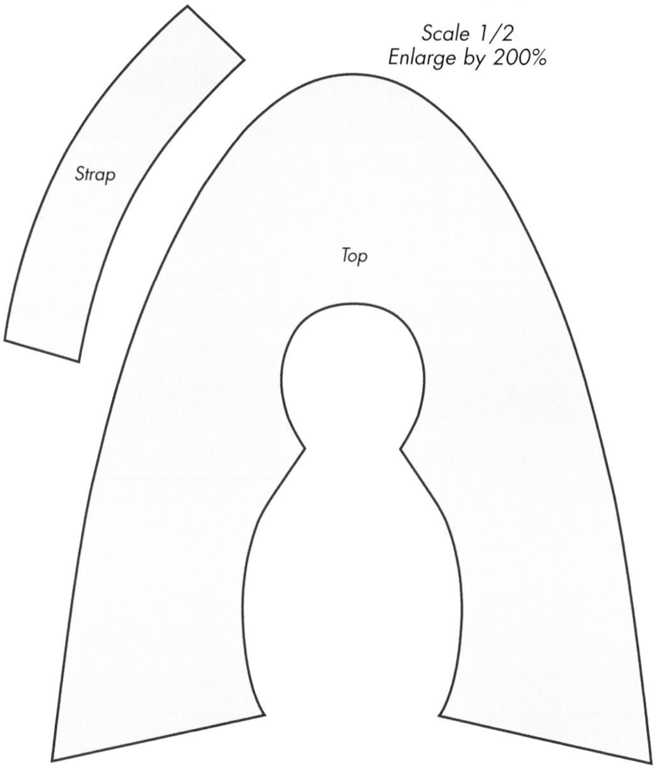

Strap

Top

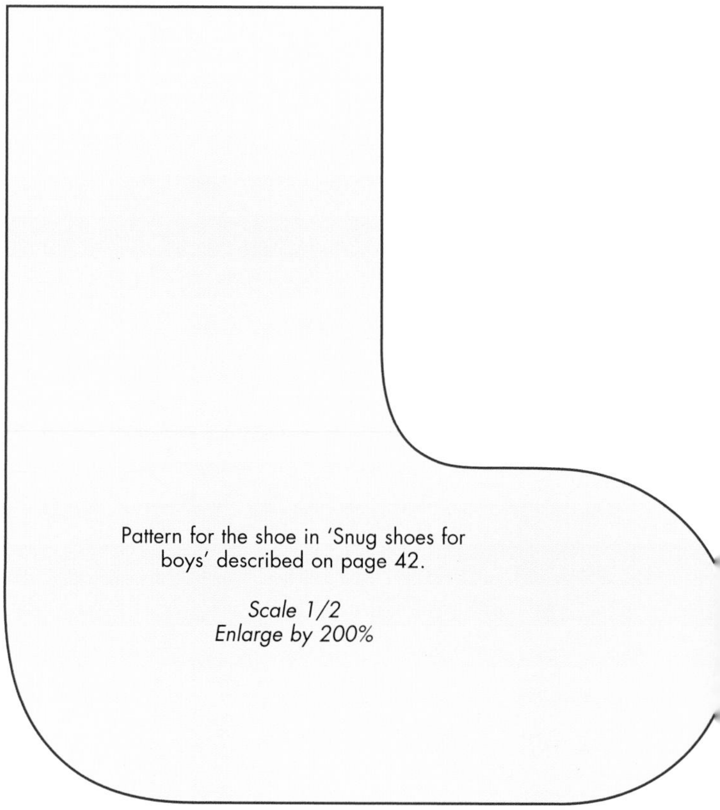

Pattern
for gingerbread
man silhouette for bag **A**
described on page 49.

Scale 1/2
Enlarge by 200%

Half-pattern for the 'Silk bag'
described on page 39.

Scale 1/4
Enlarge by 400%

Pattern for the shoe in 'Snug shoes for
boys' described on page 42.

Scale 1/2
Enlarge by 200%

Fold of fabric

Motif for the rosette described on page 59.

Scale 1/2
Enlarge by 200%

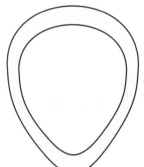

Patterns for the two petals used in the 'Flower brooches' described on pages 52 and 58.

Scale 1/2
Enlarge by 200%

Actual size pattern for the flower used for the 'Ring' described on page 54.

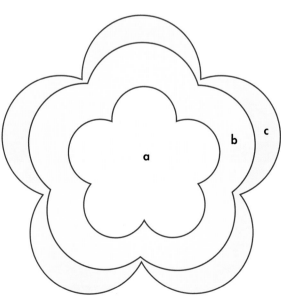

a b c

Actual size patterns for the flowers used for the 'Shoe jewel' and 'Fingerless gloves' described on page 55.

Contents

First published in Great Britain 2007 by Search Press Limited,
Wellwood, North Farm Road, Tunbridge Wells, Kent TN2 3DR

Originally published in France 2006 by Éditions Didier Carpentier
Copyright © Éditions Didier Carpentier

English translation by Cicero Translations
English translation copyright © Search Press Limited 2007
English edition edited and typeset by GreenGate Publishing Services, Tonbridge, Kent

ISBN-10: 1-84448-282-0

ISBN-13: 978-1-84448-282-5